This Book Belongs to :

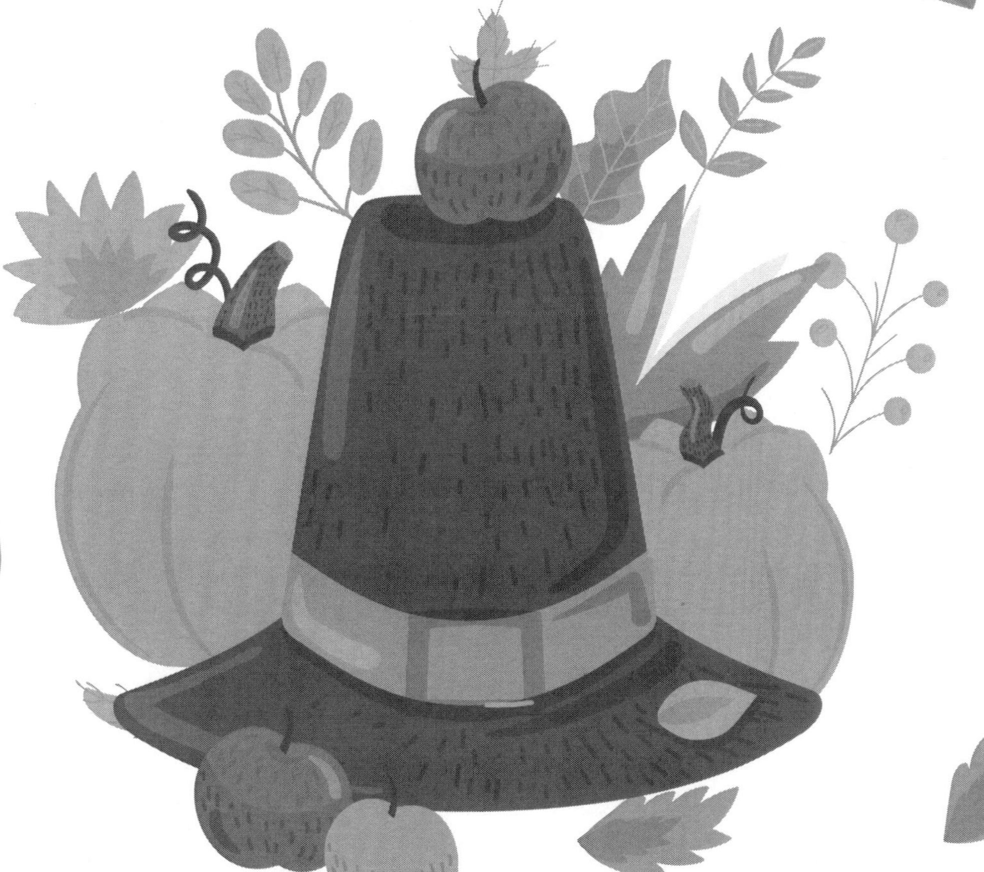

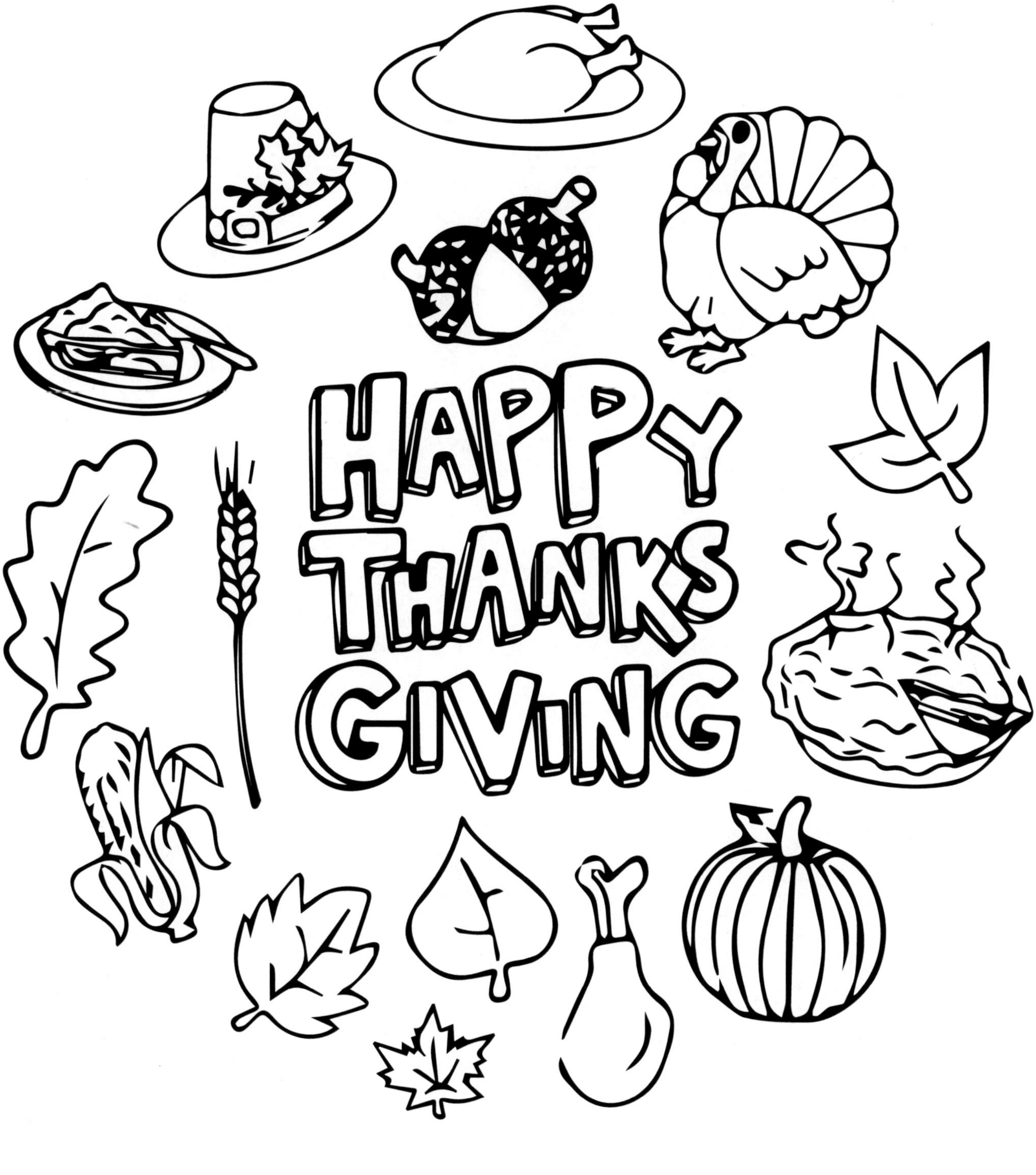
HAPPY
THANKS
GIVING

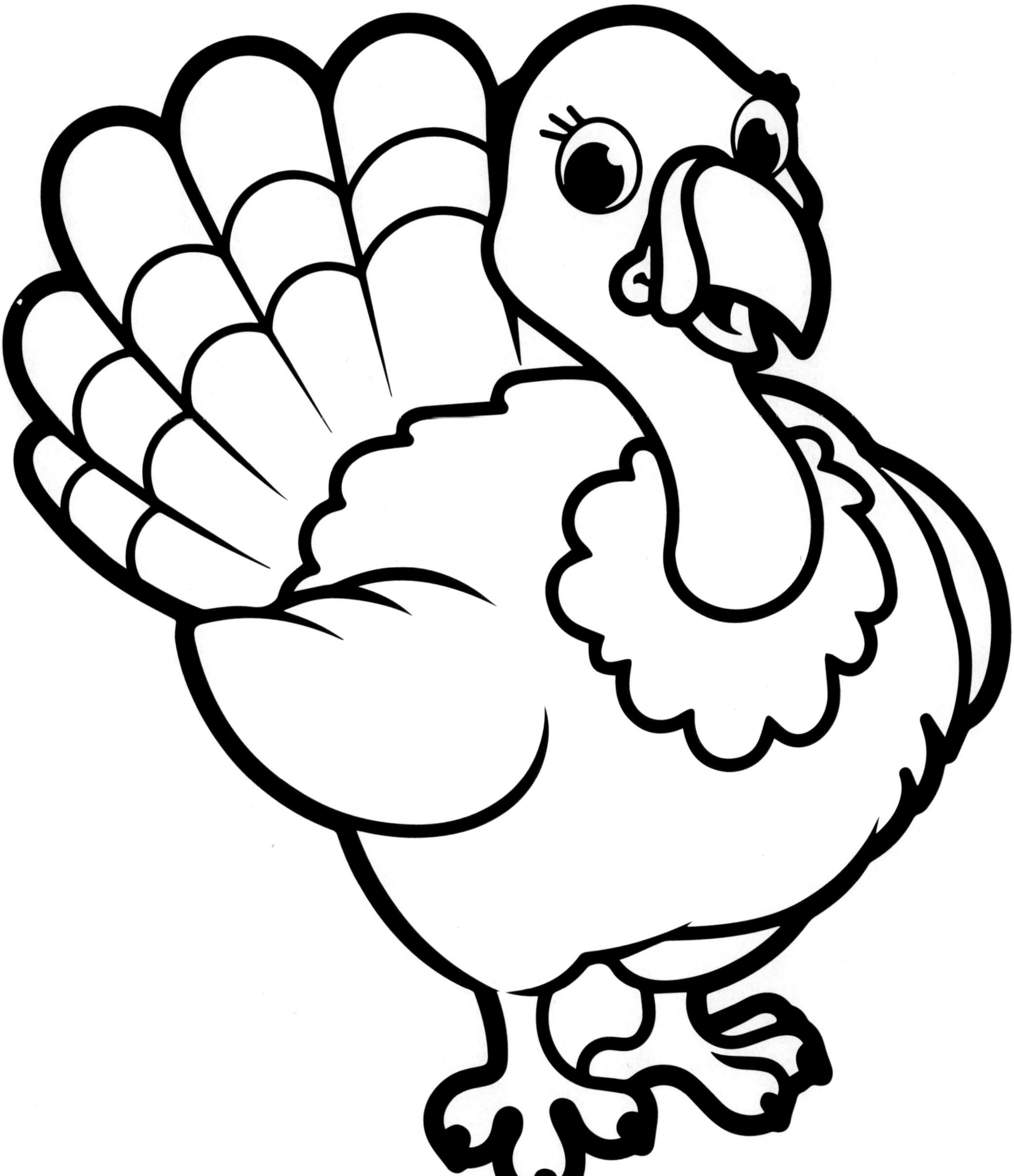

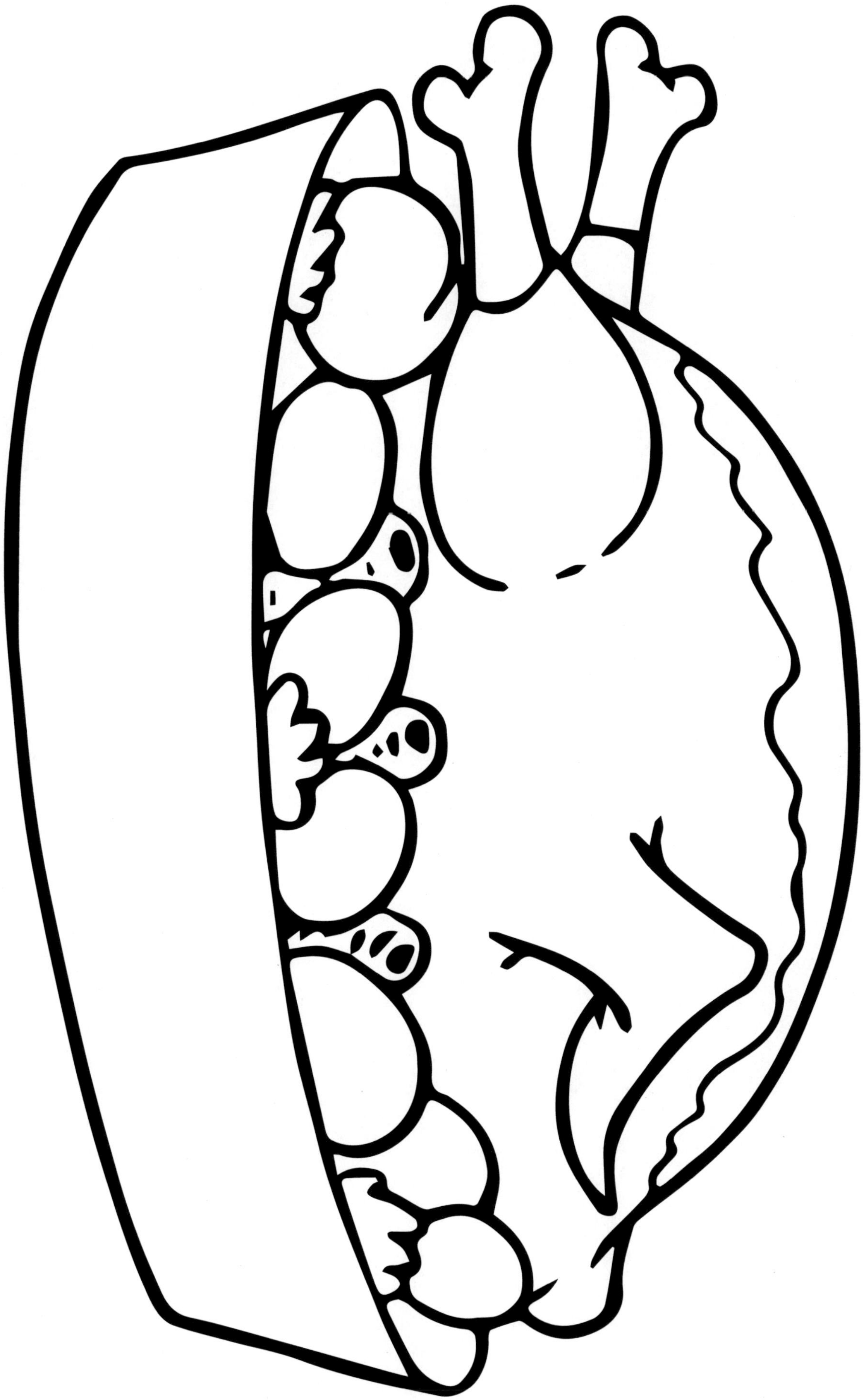

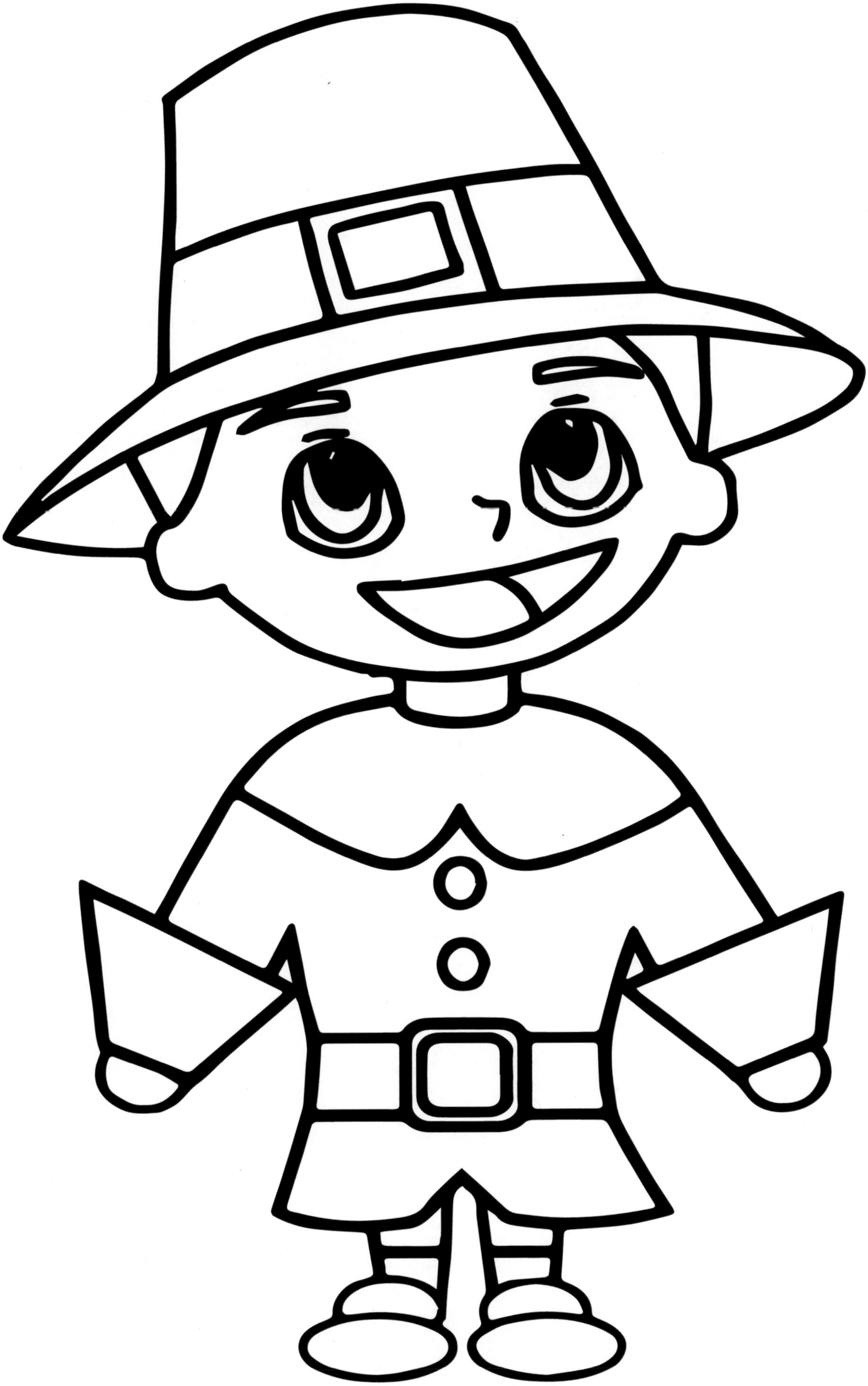

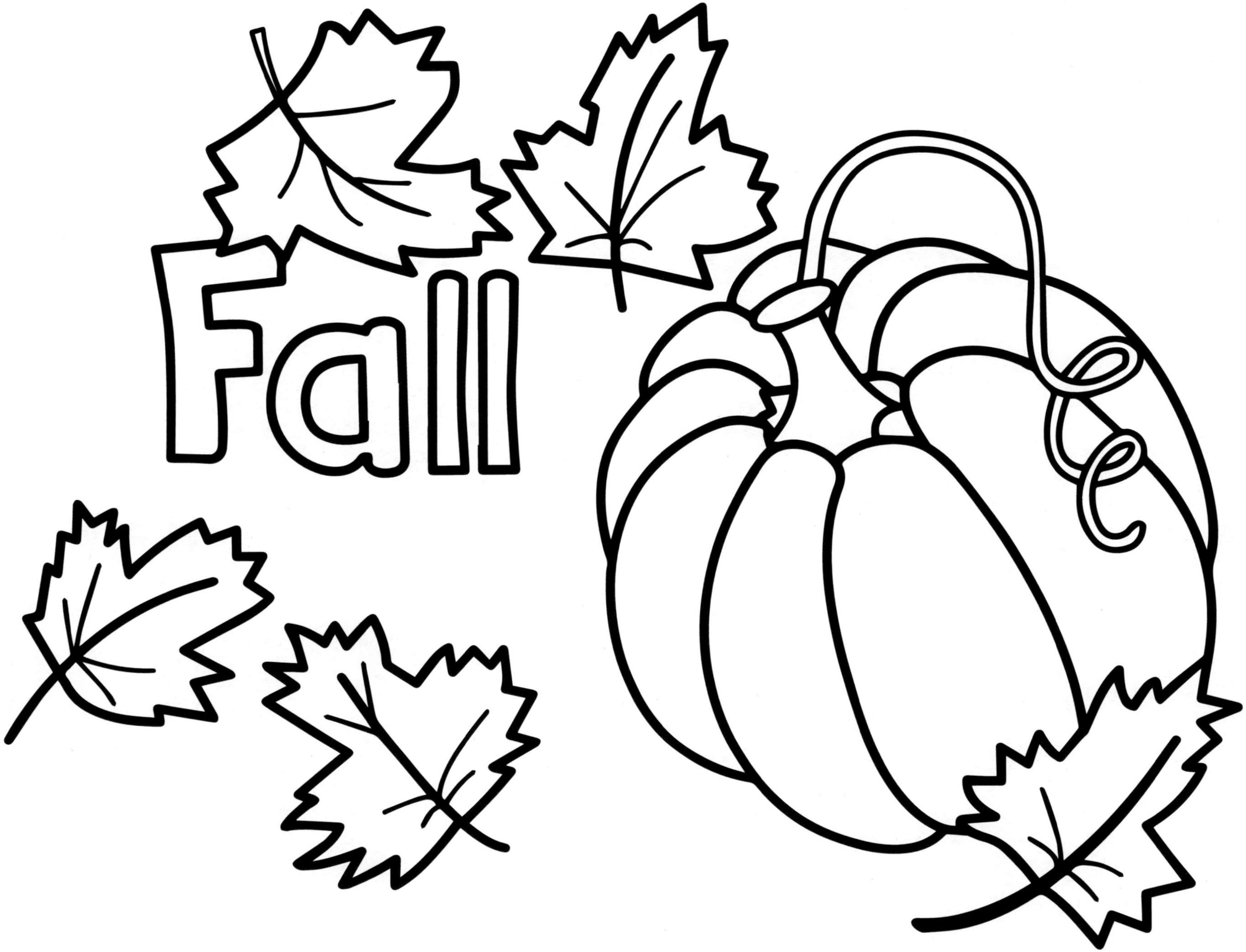
Fall

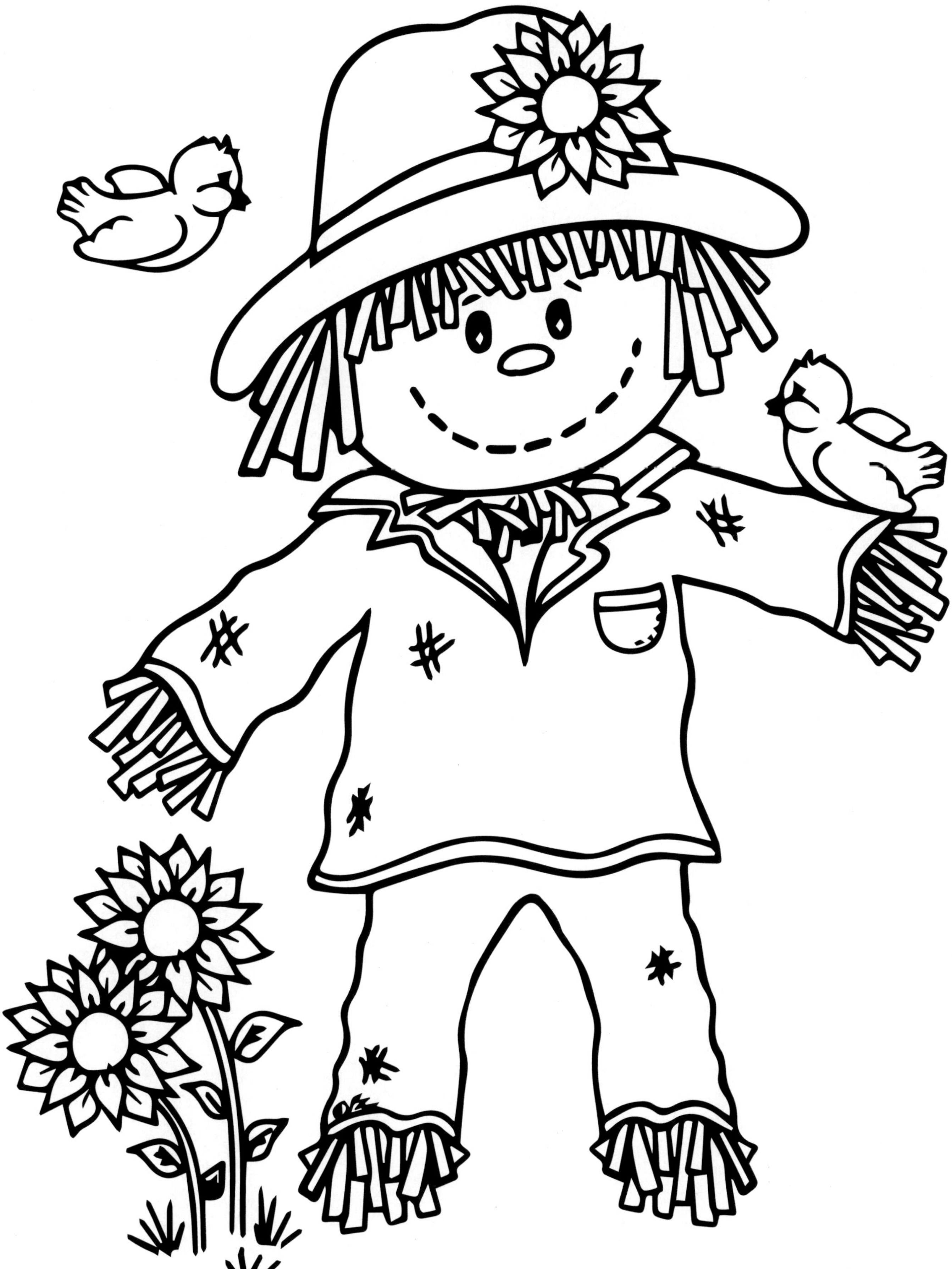

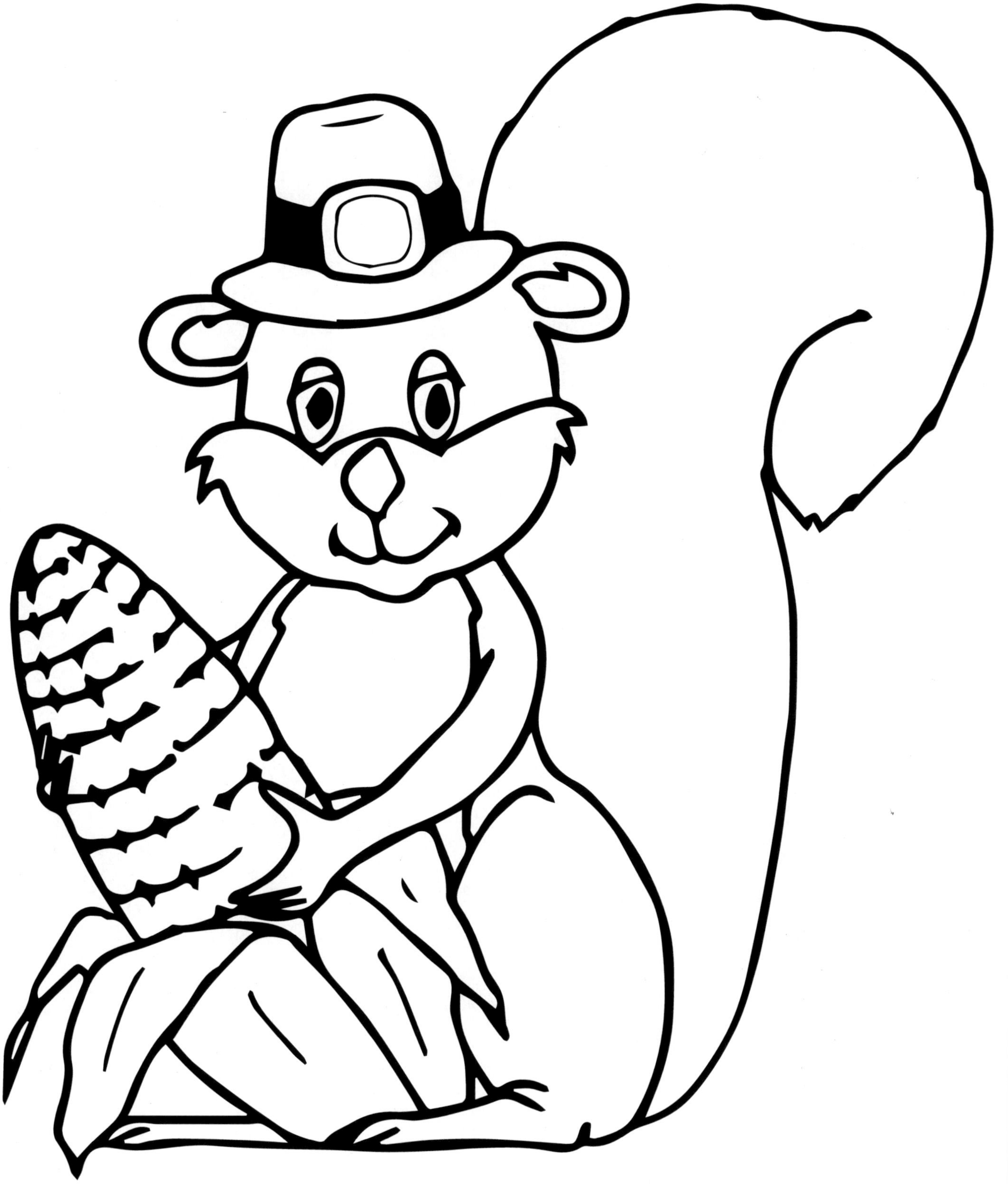

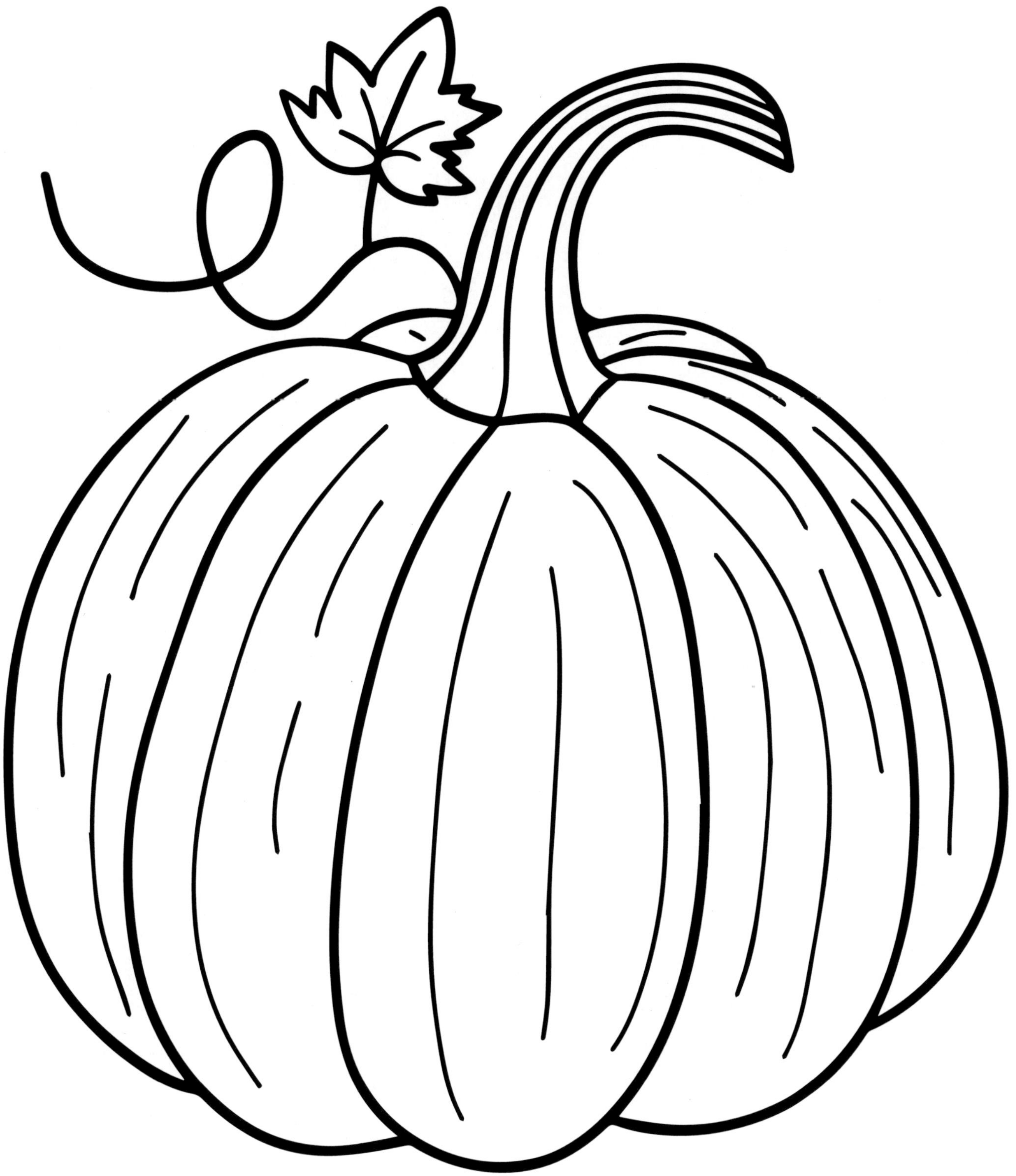

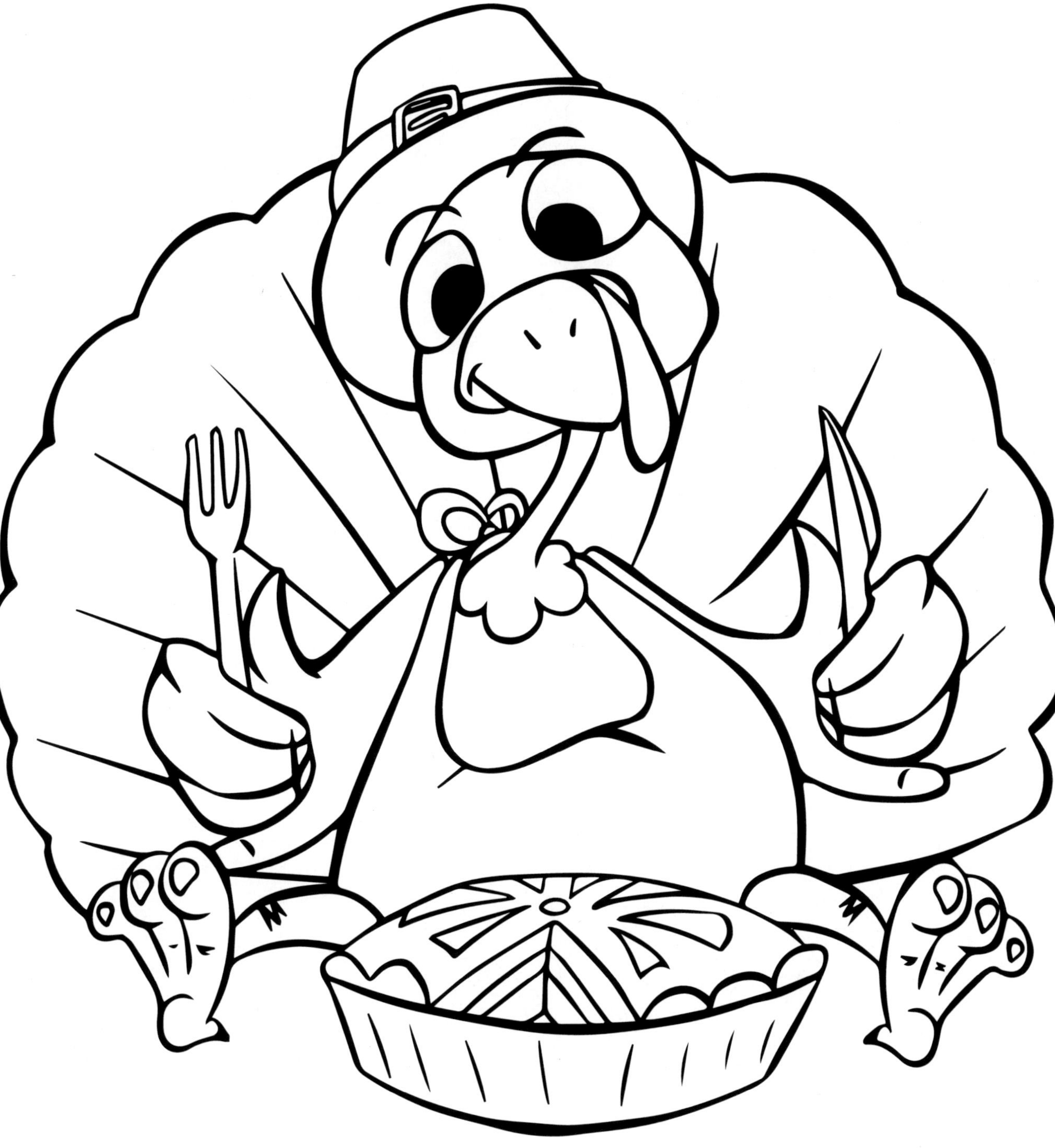

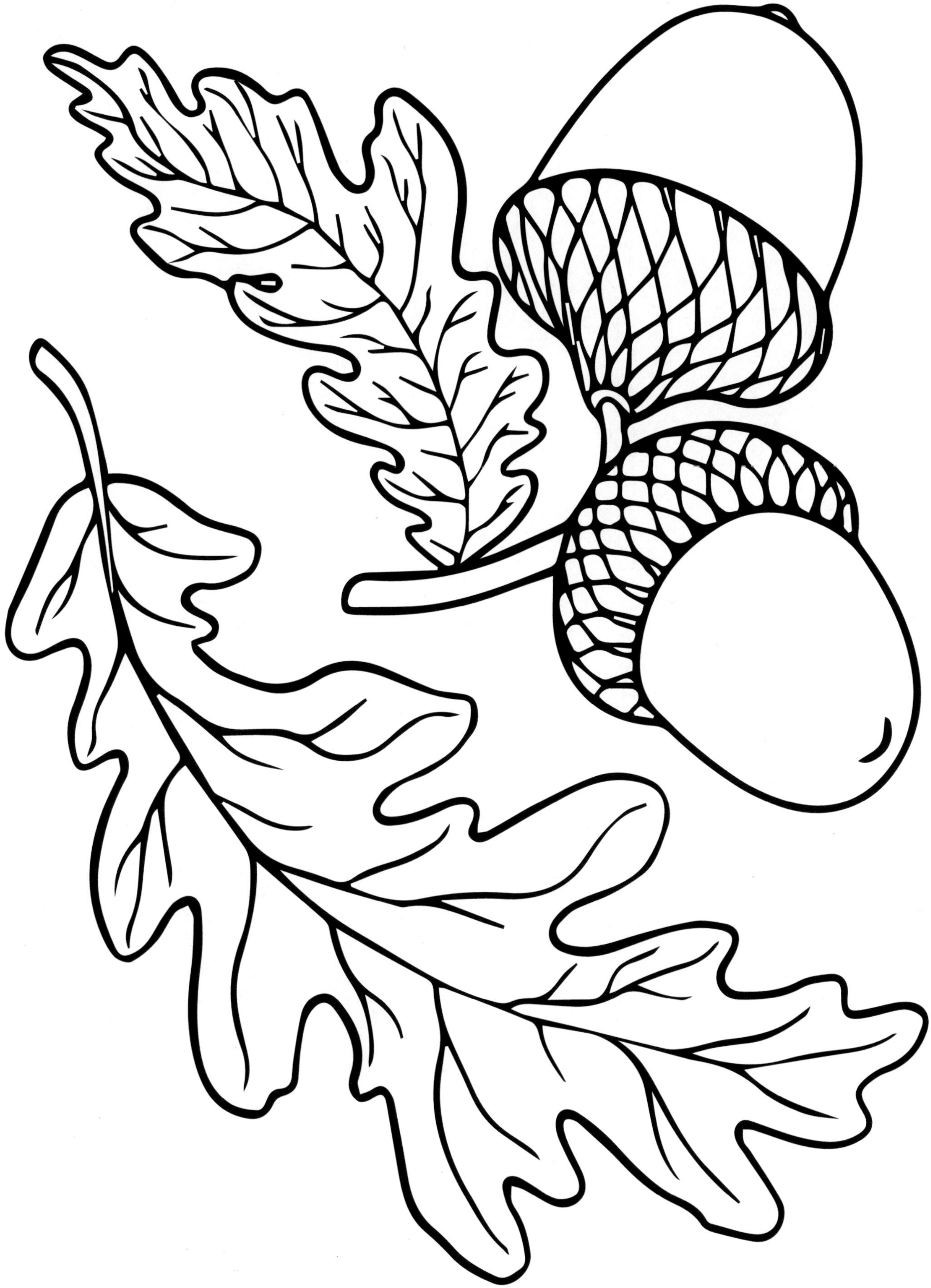

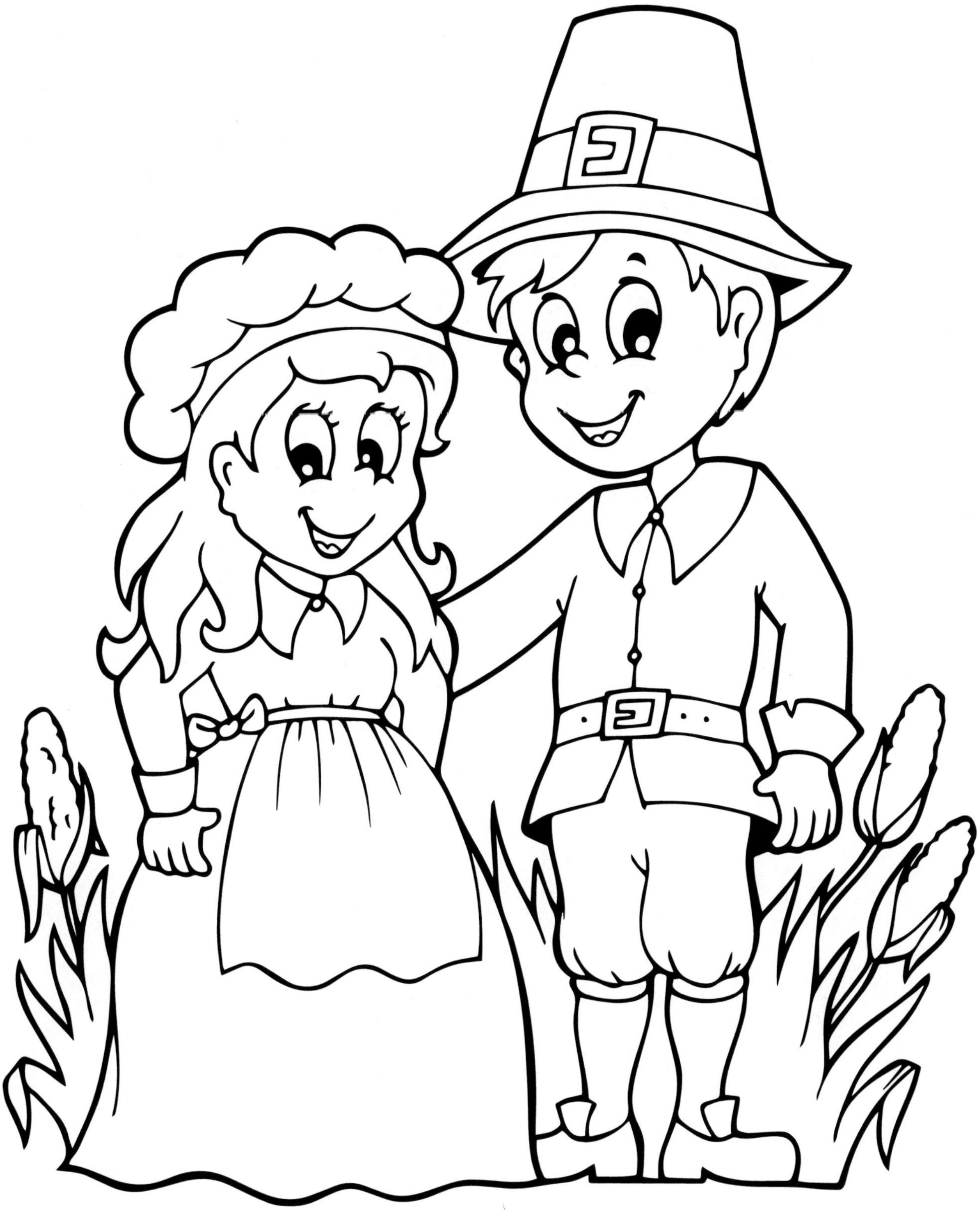

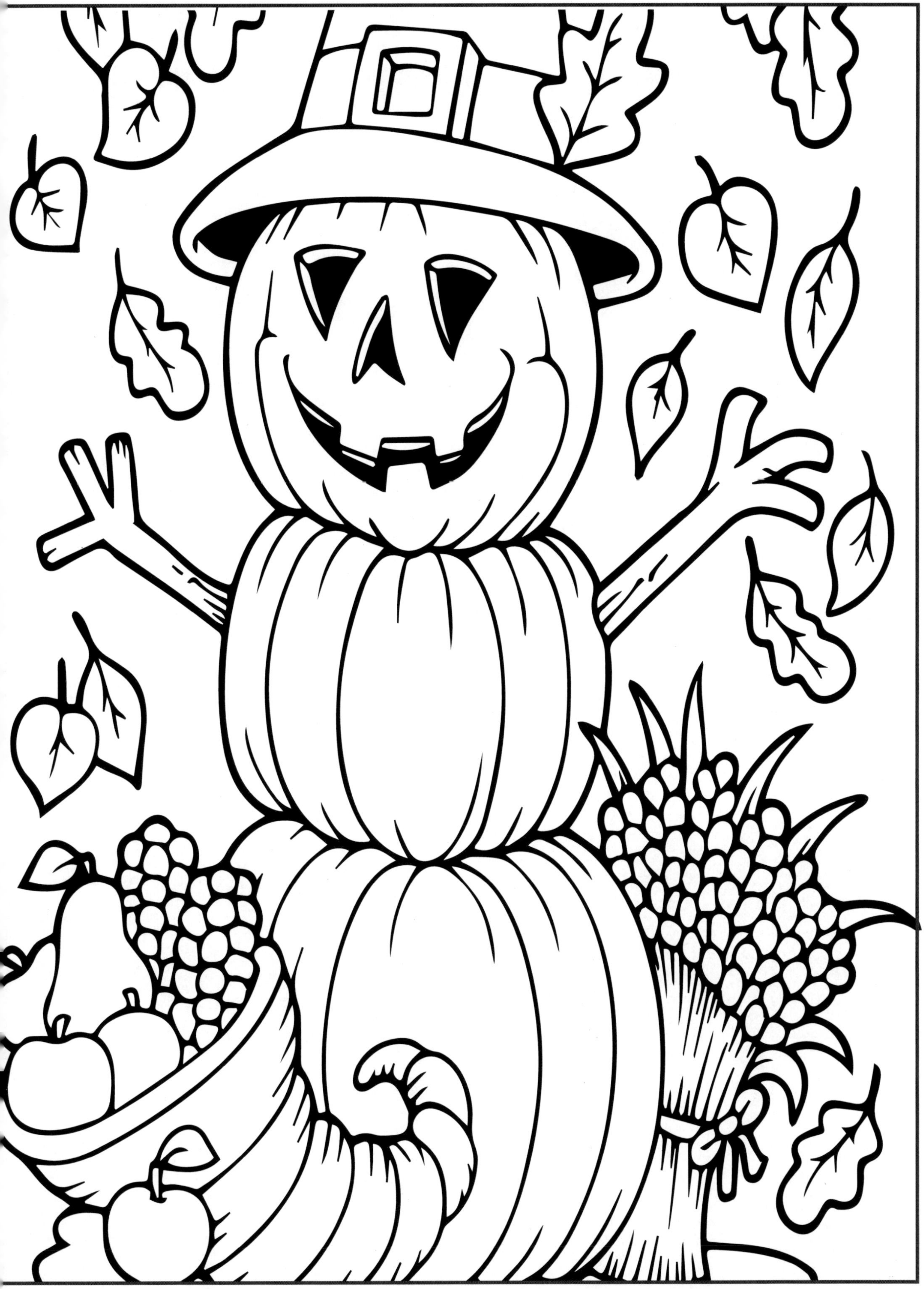

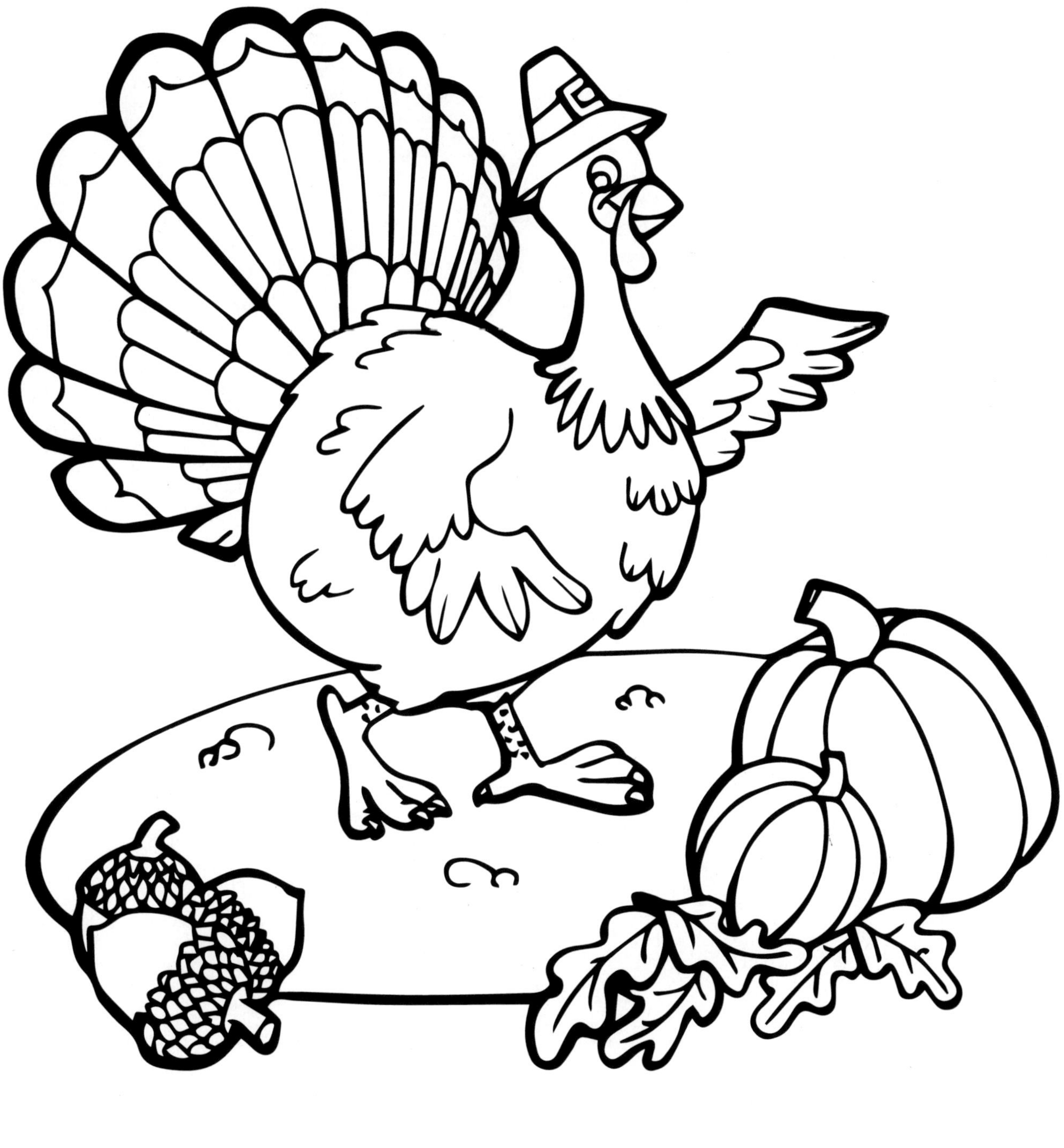

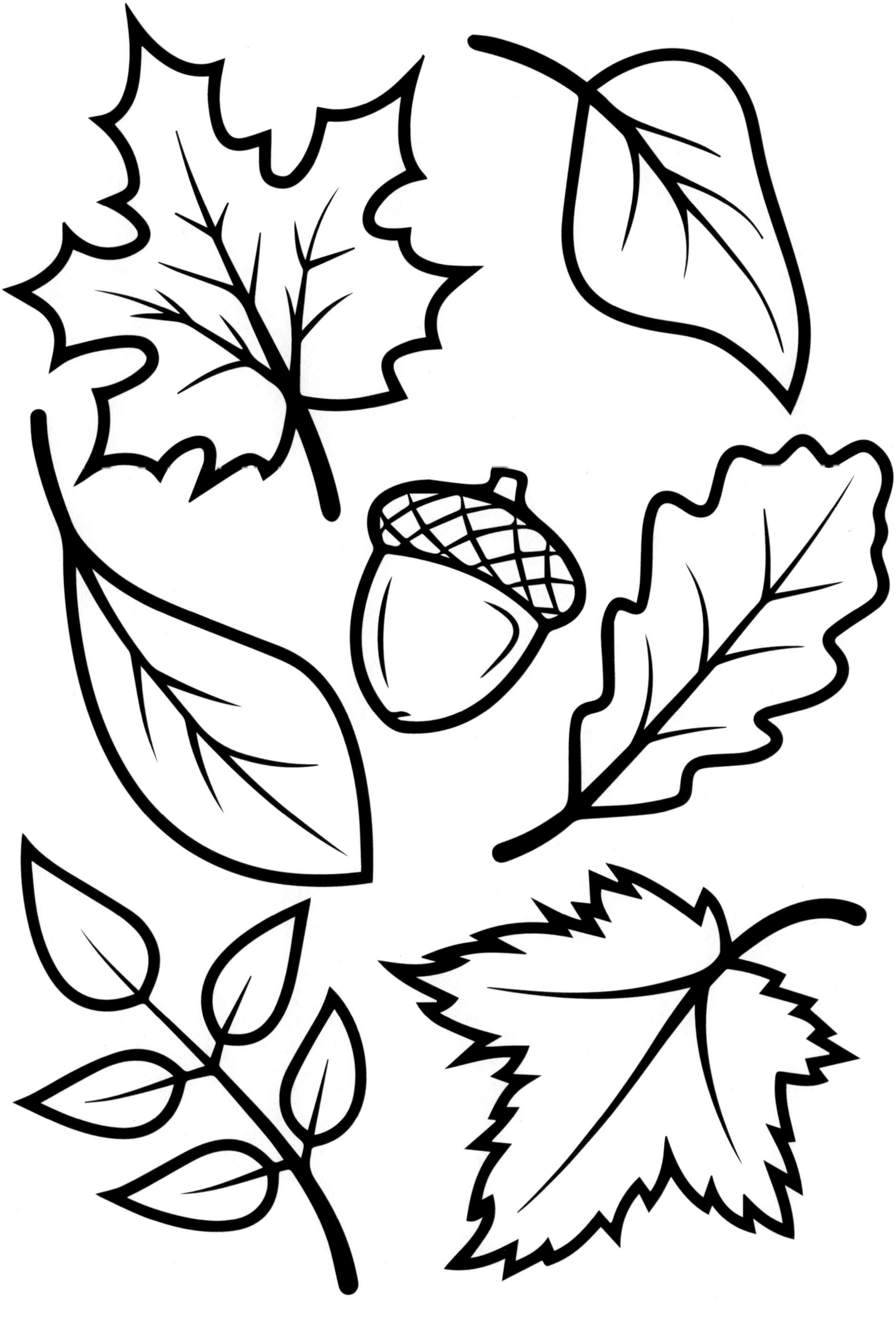

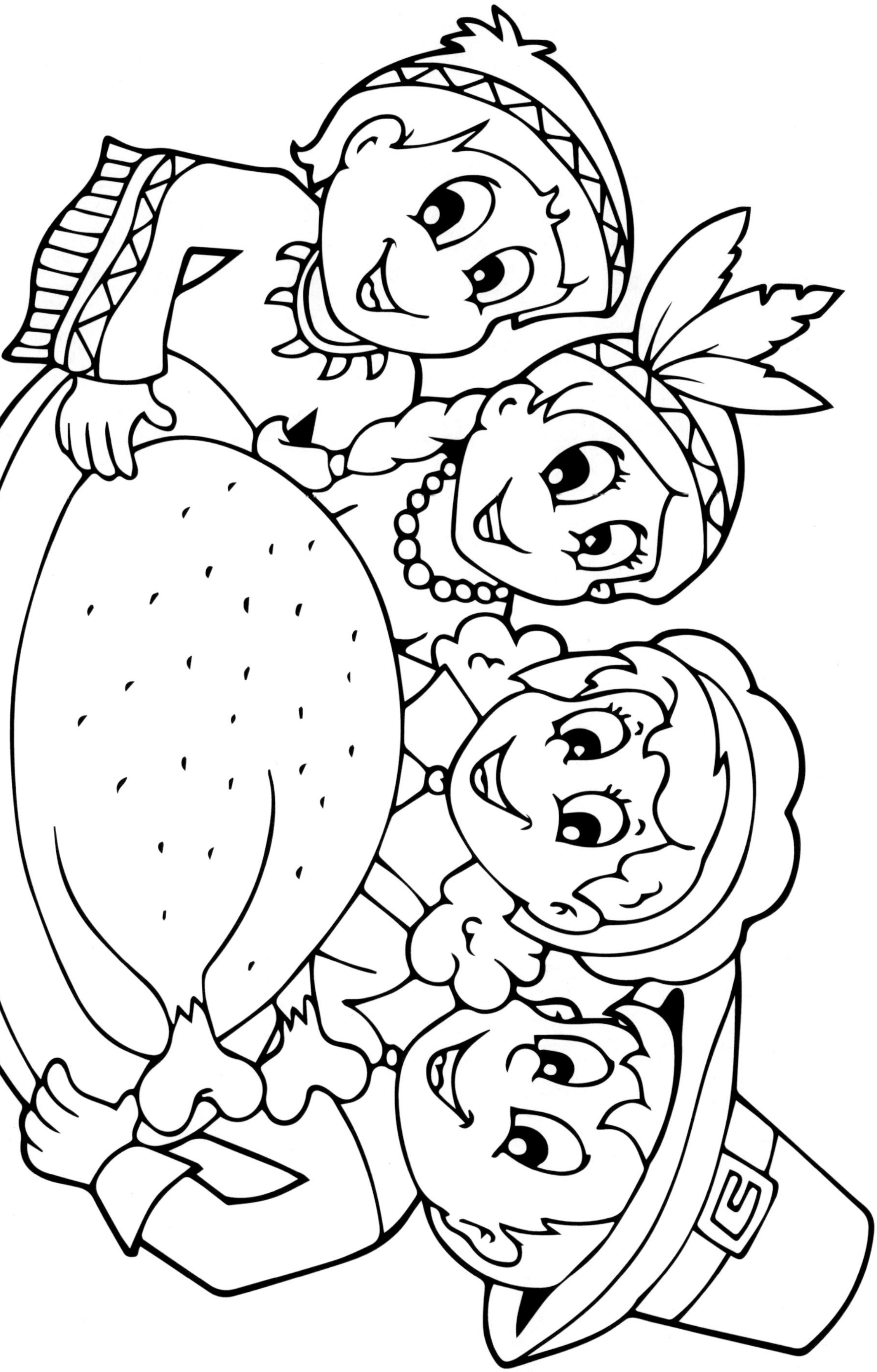

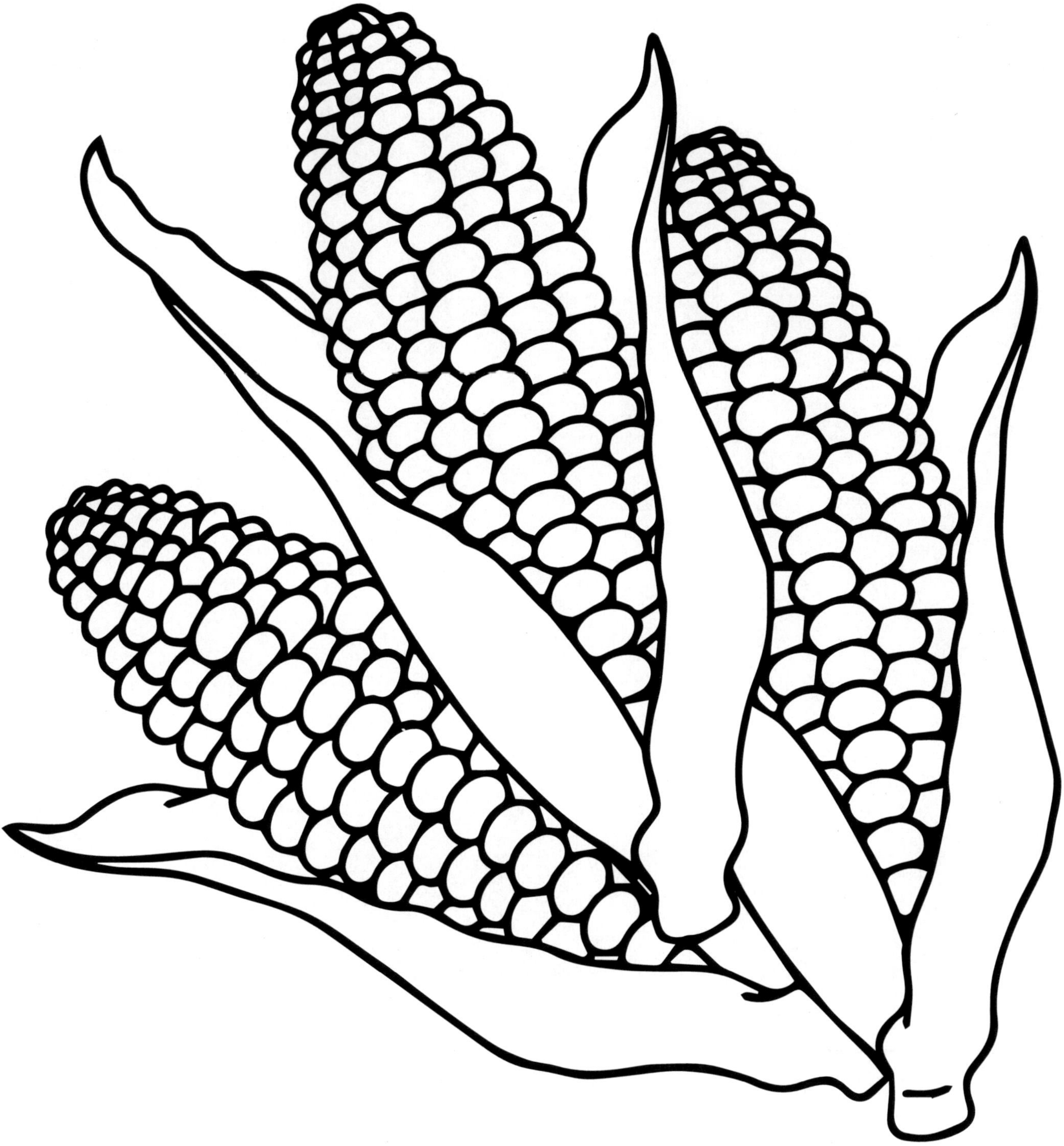

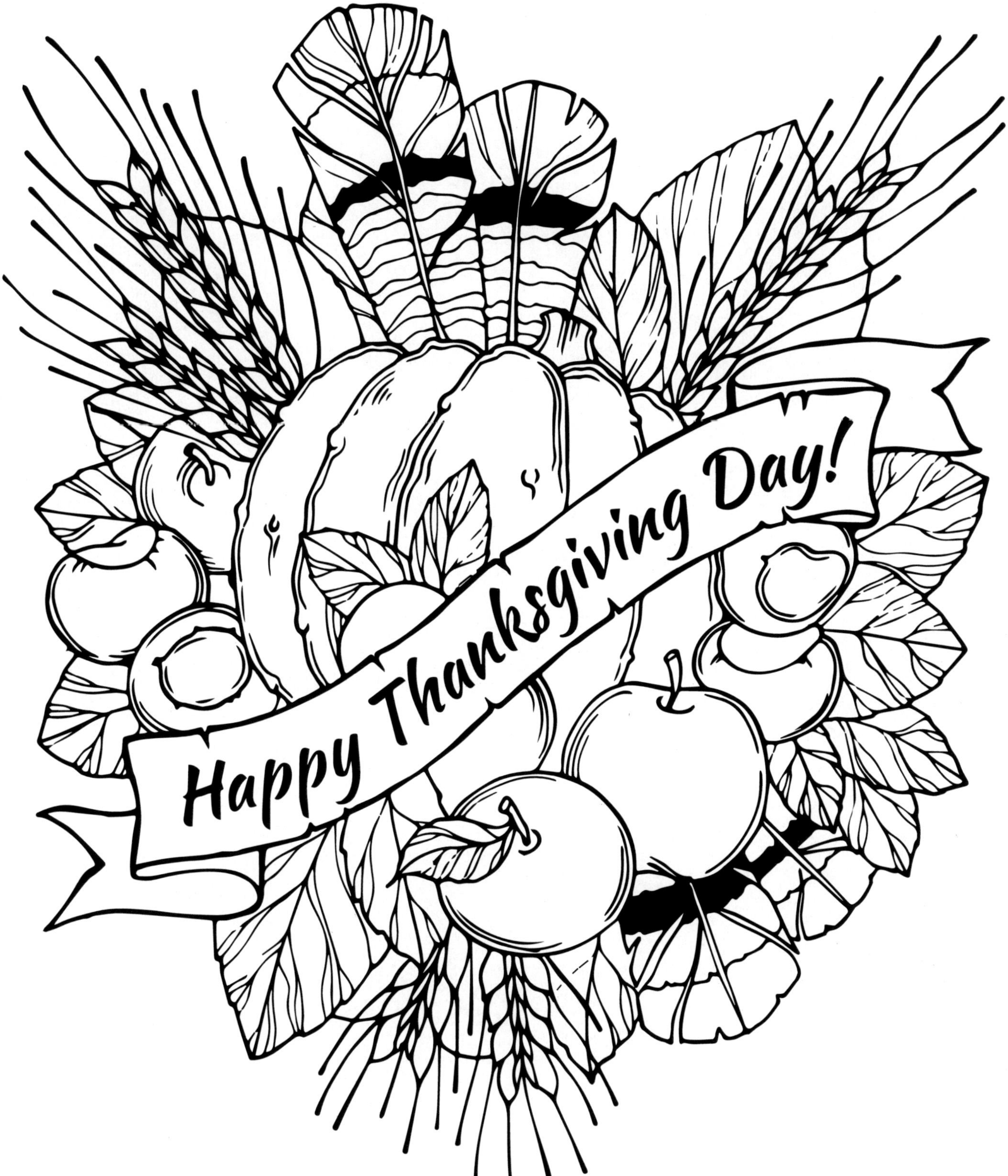
Happy Thanksgiving Day!

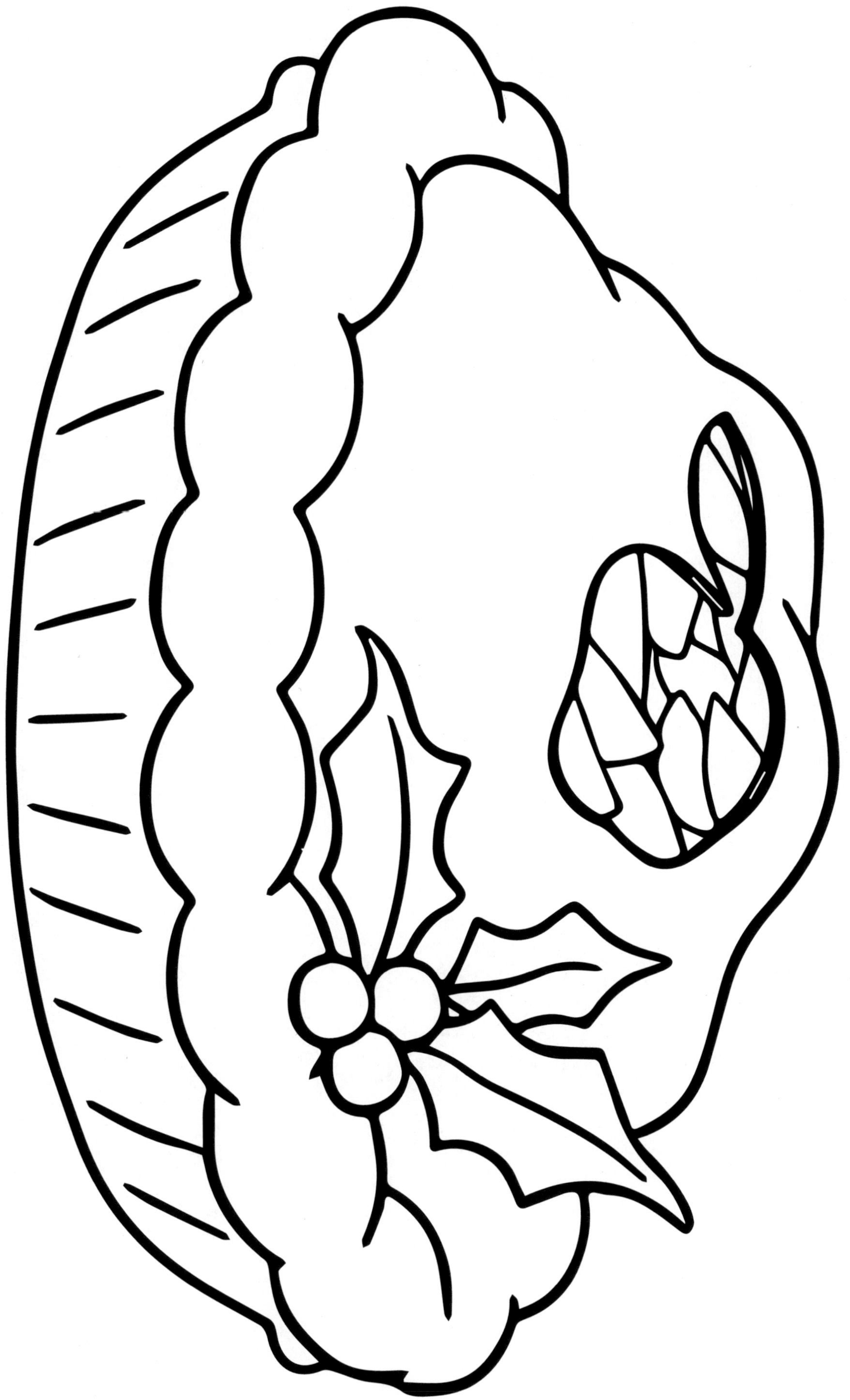

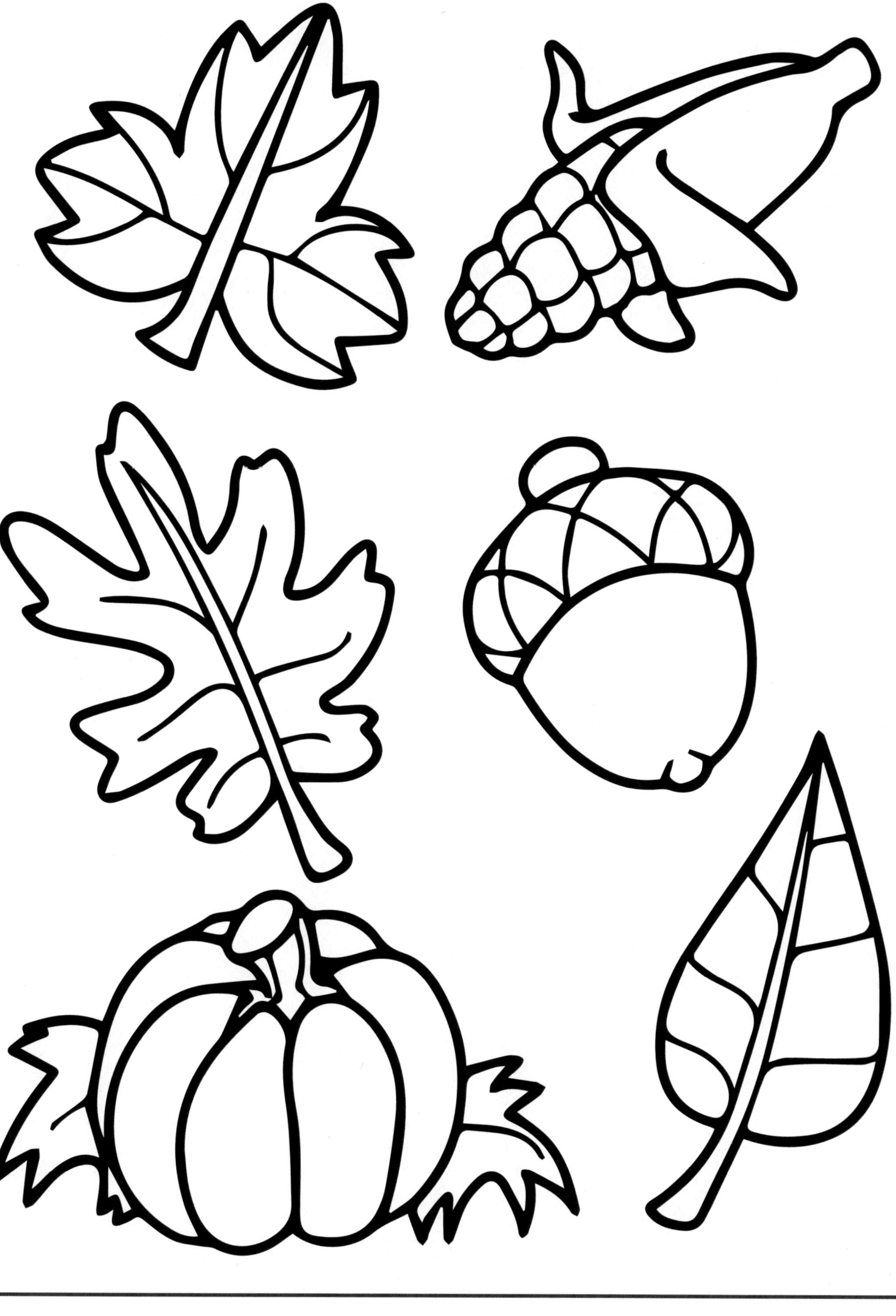

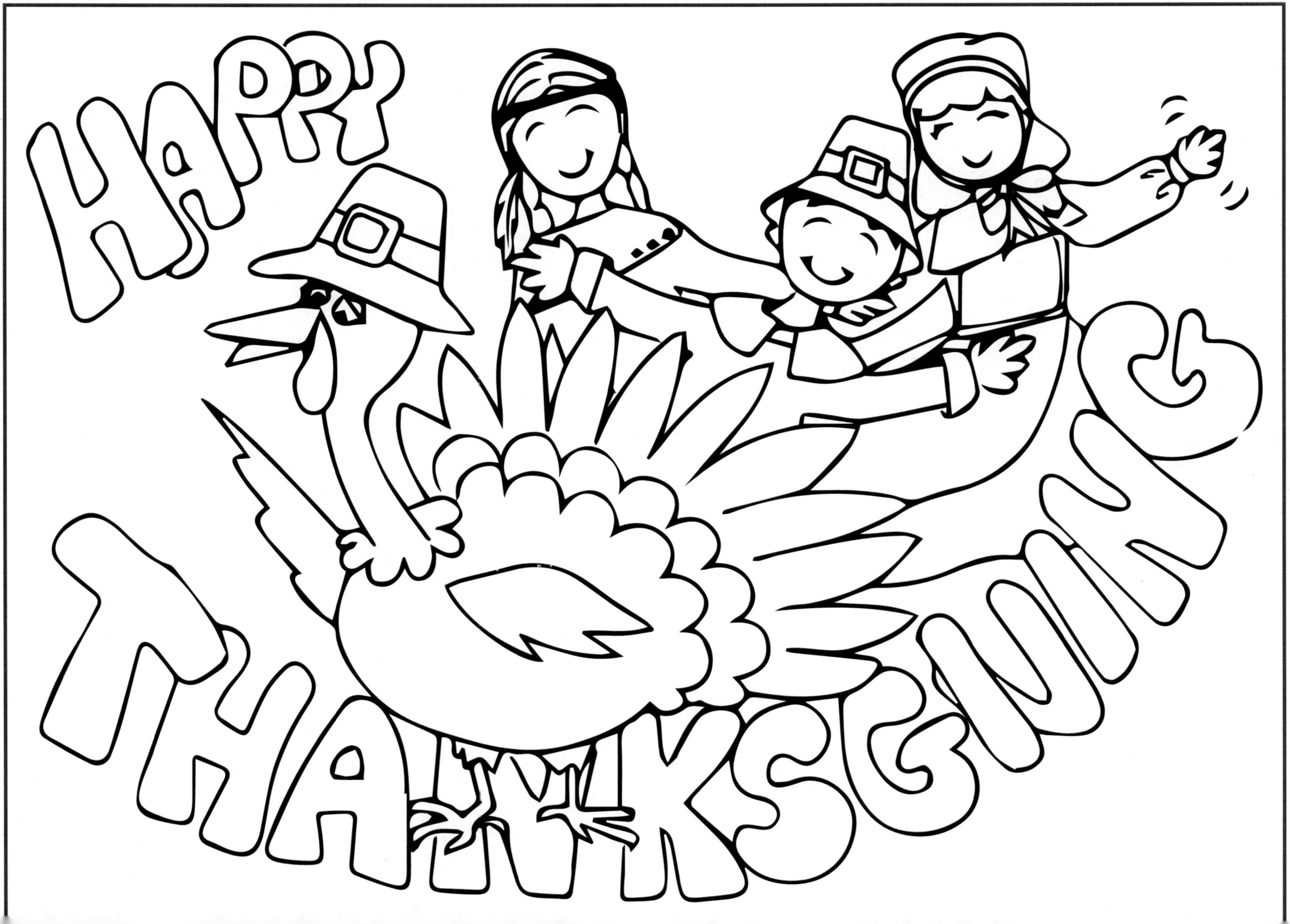
HAPPY
THANKSGIVING

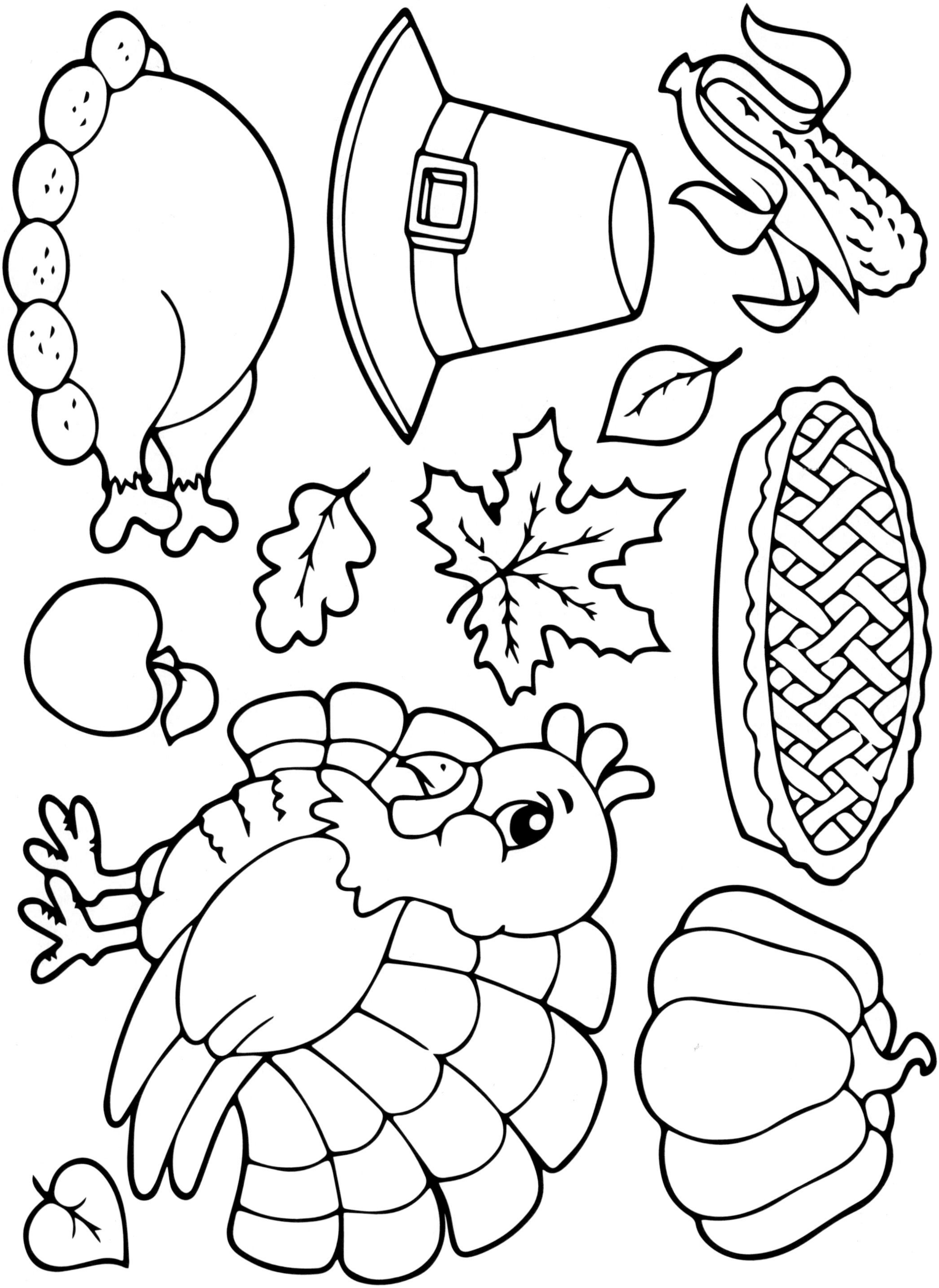

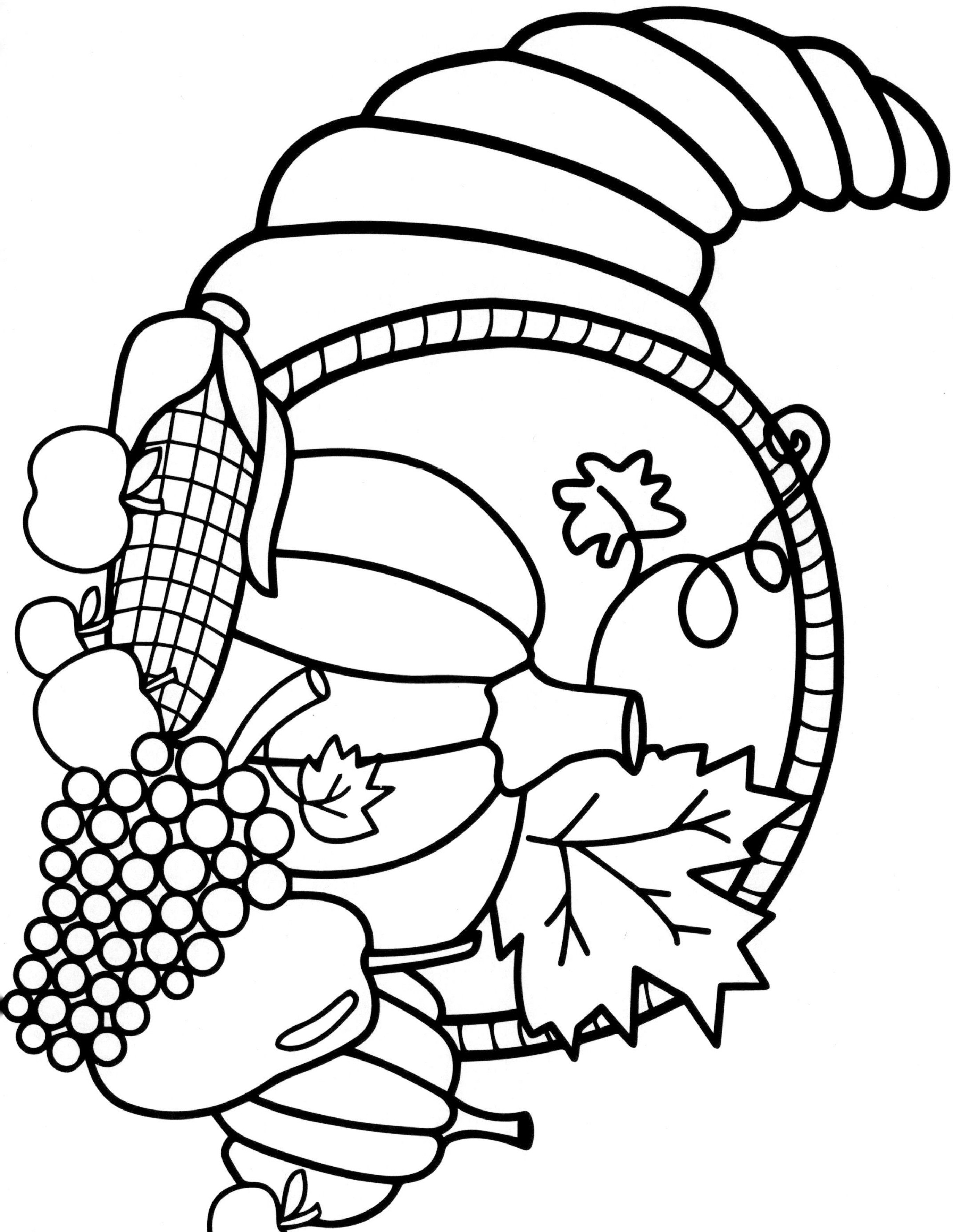

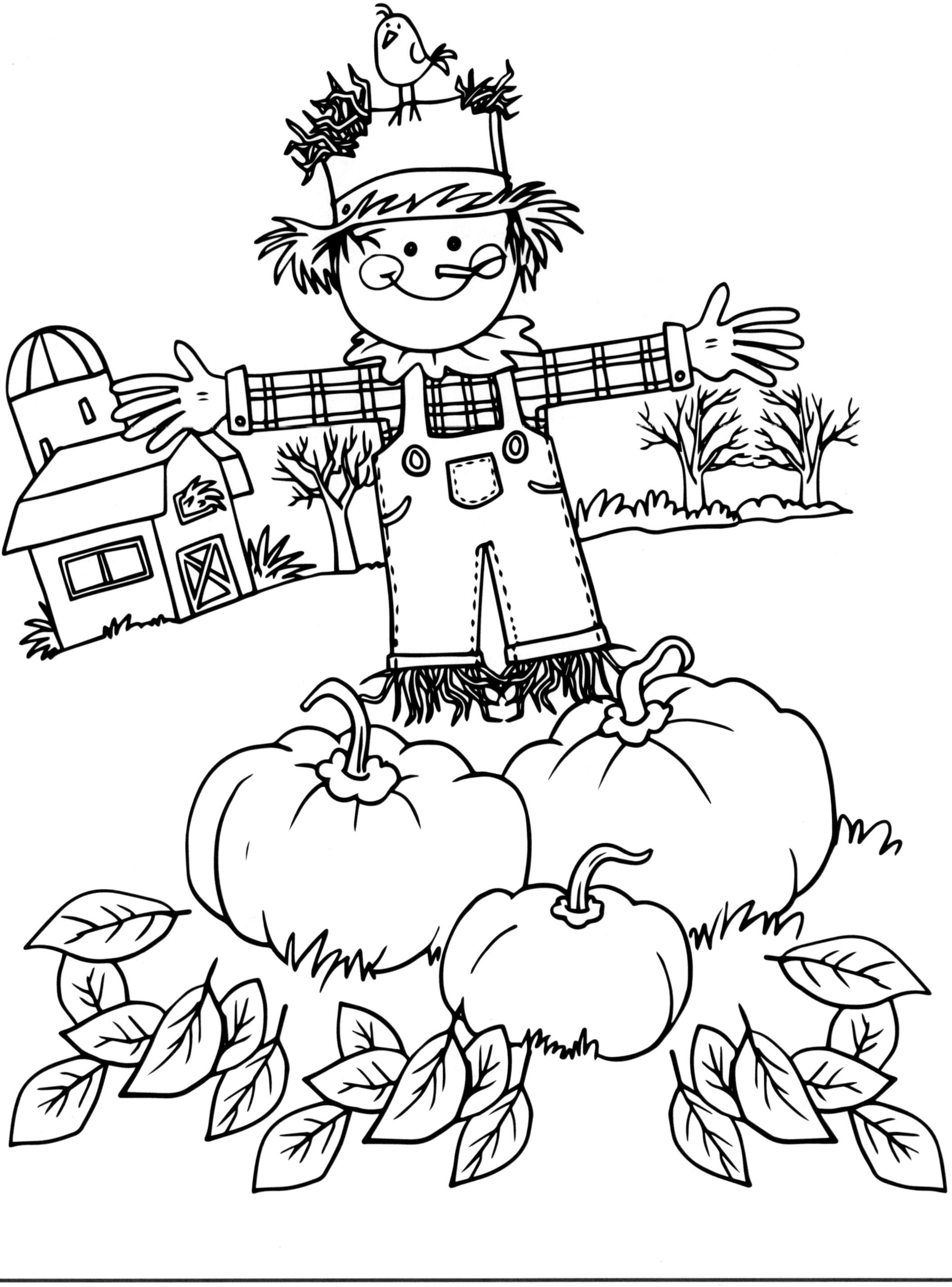

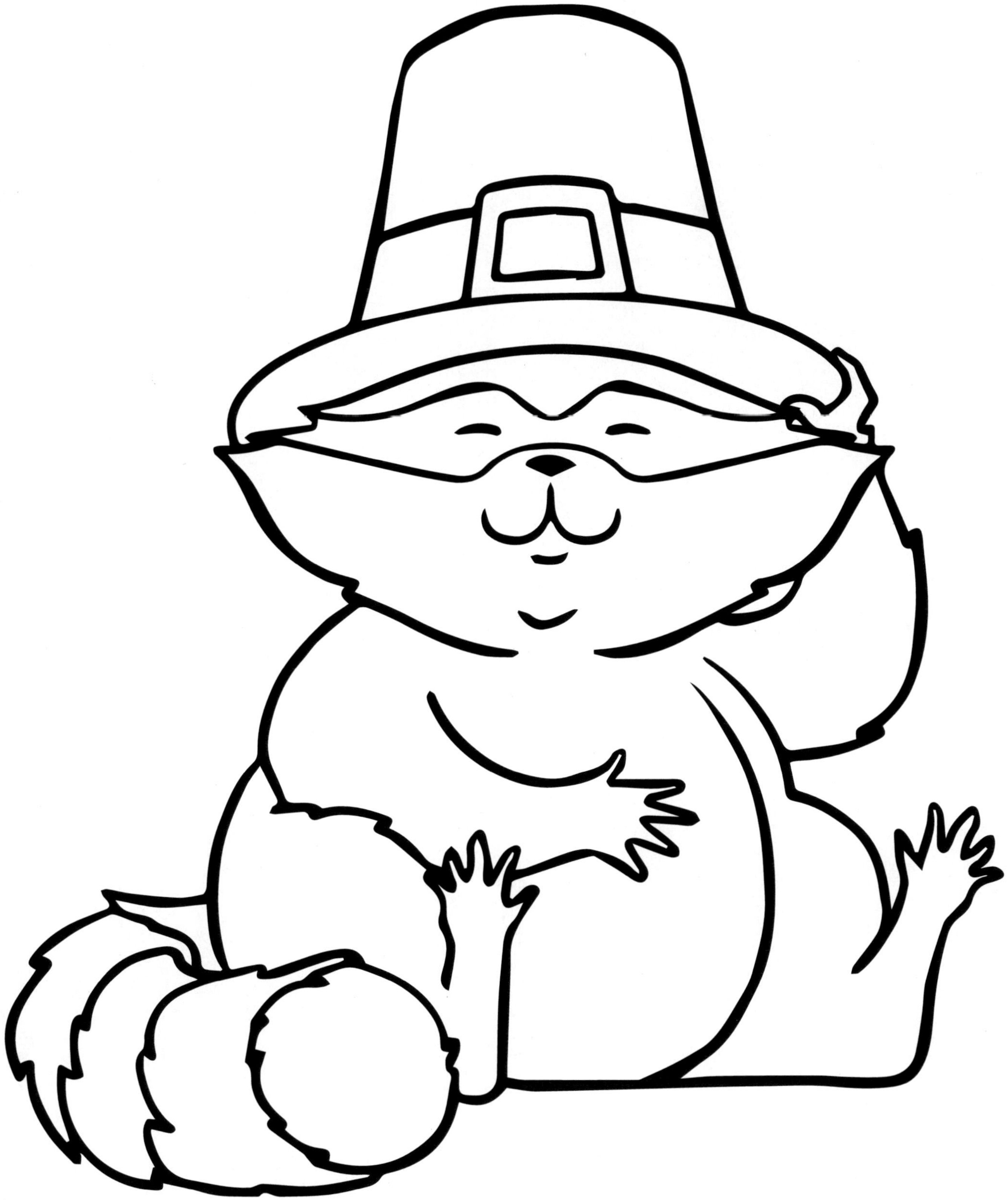

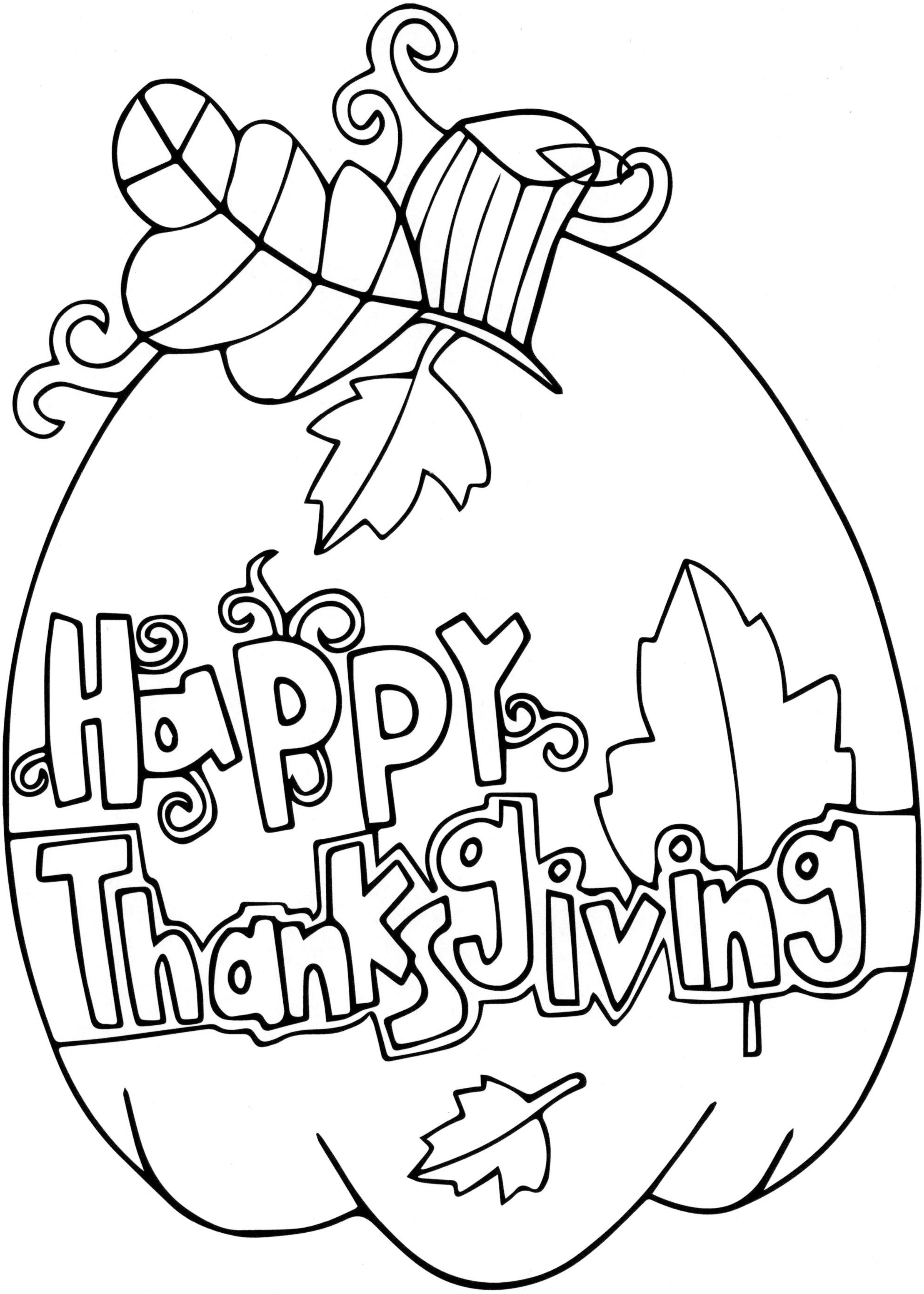
Happy Thanksgiving

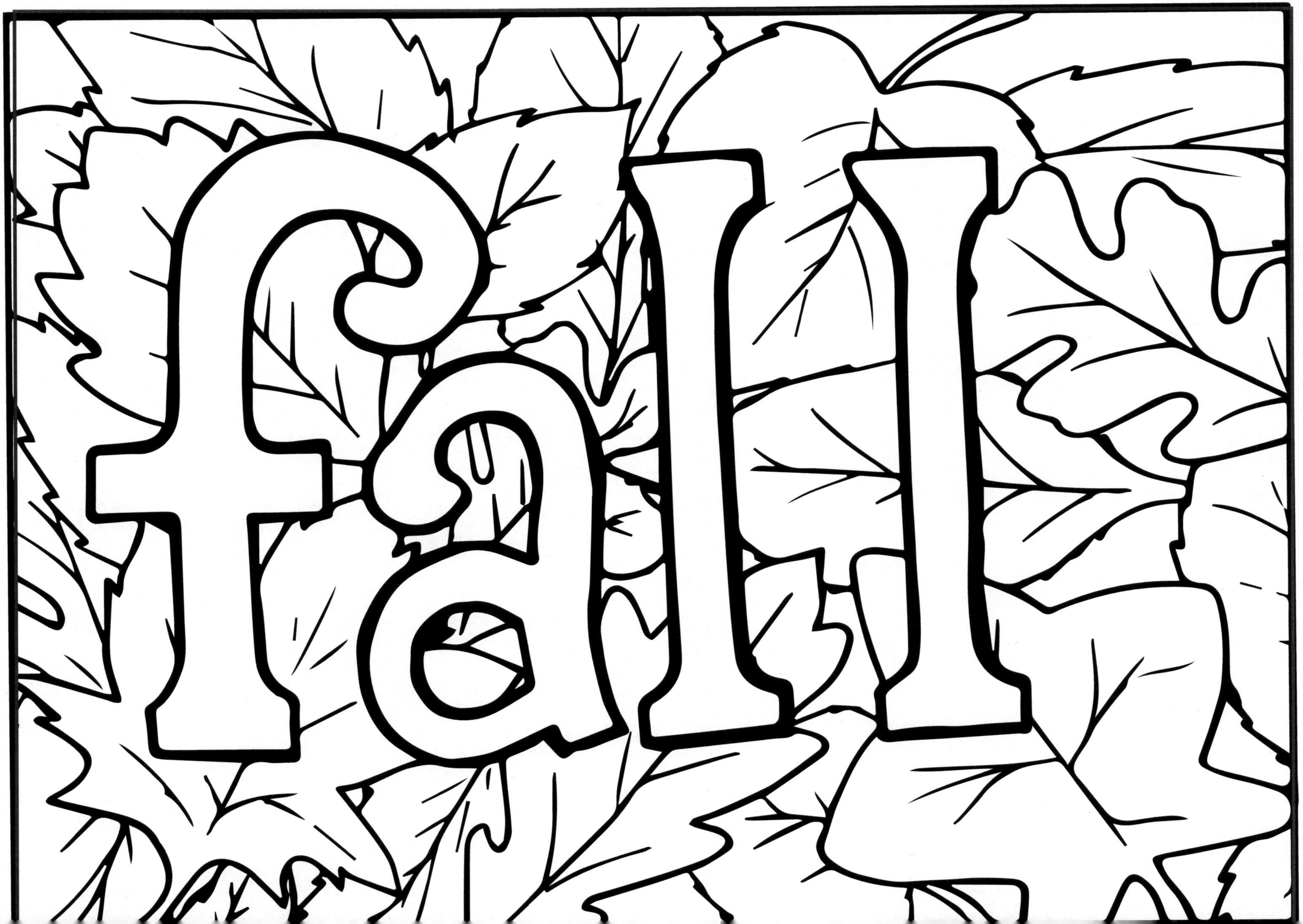
fall

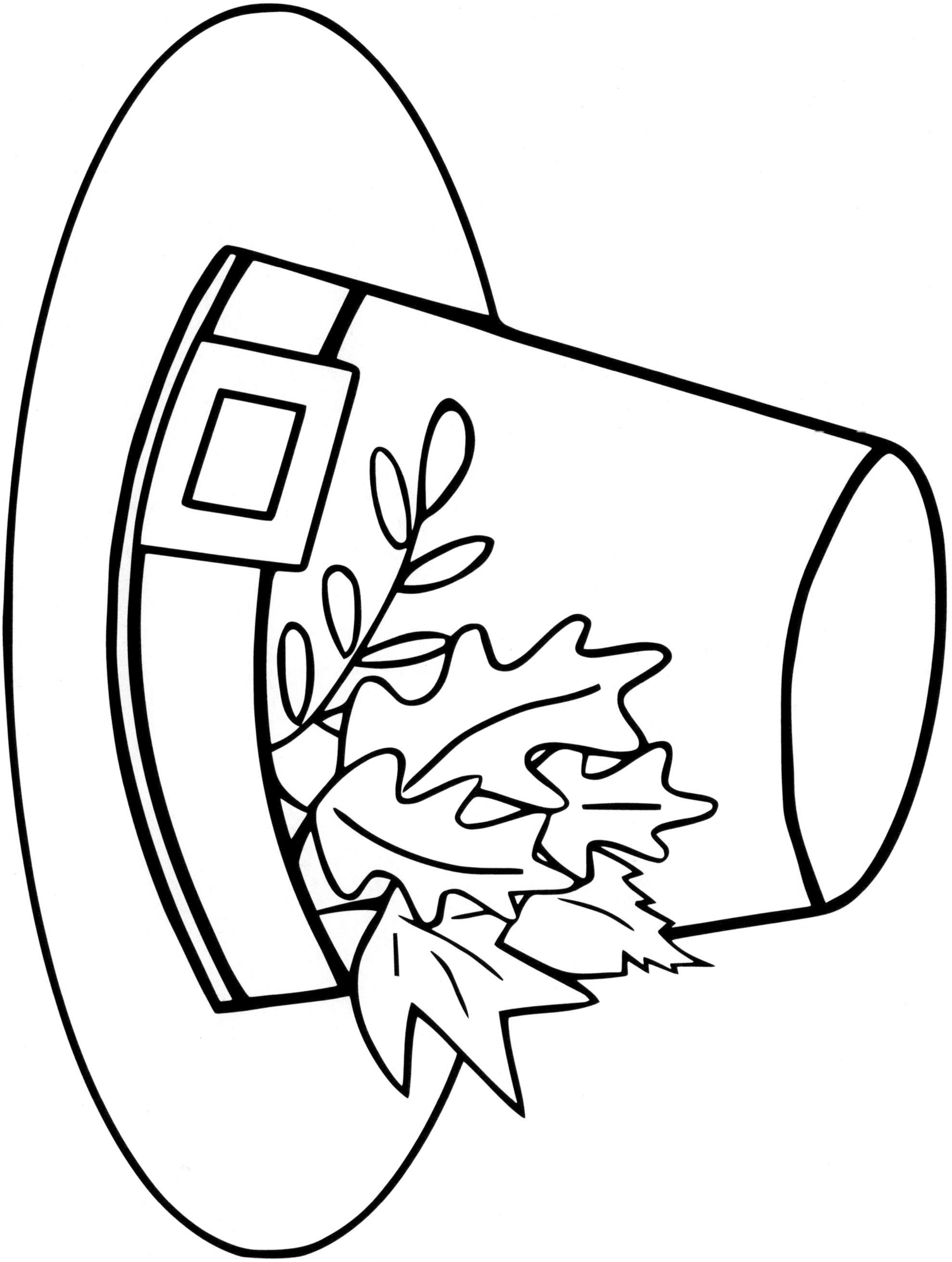

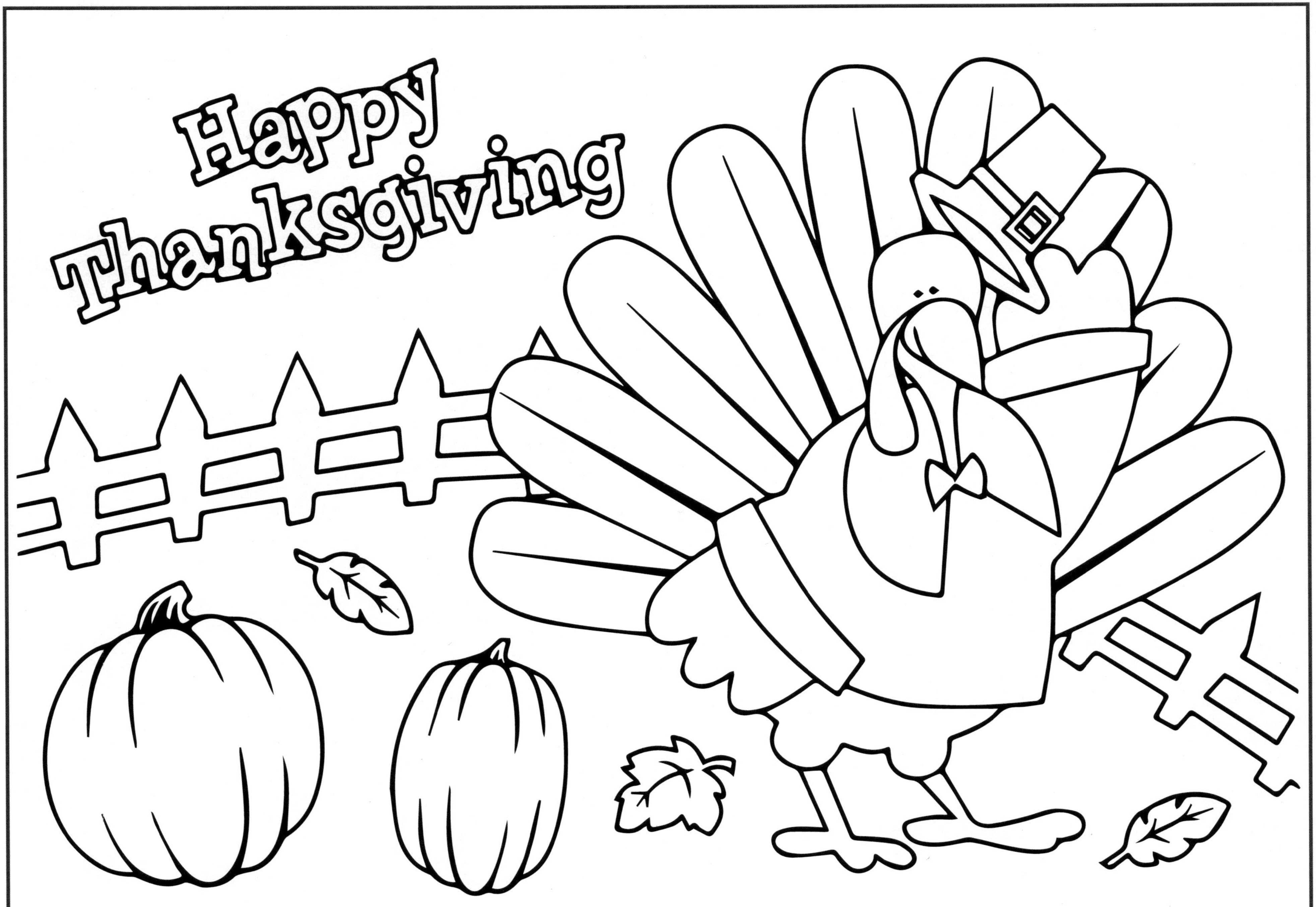
Happy Thanksgiving

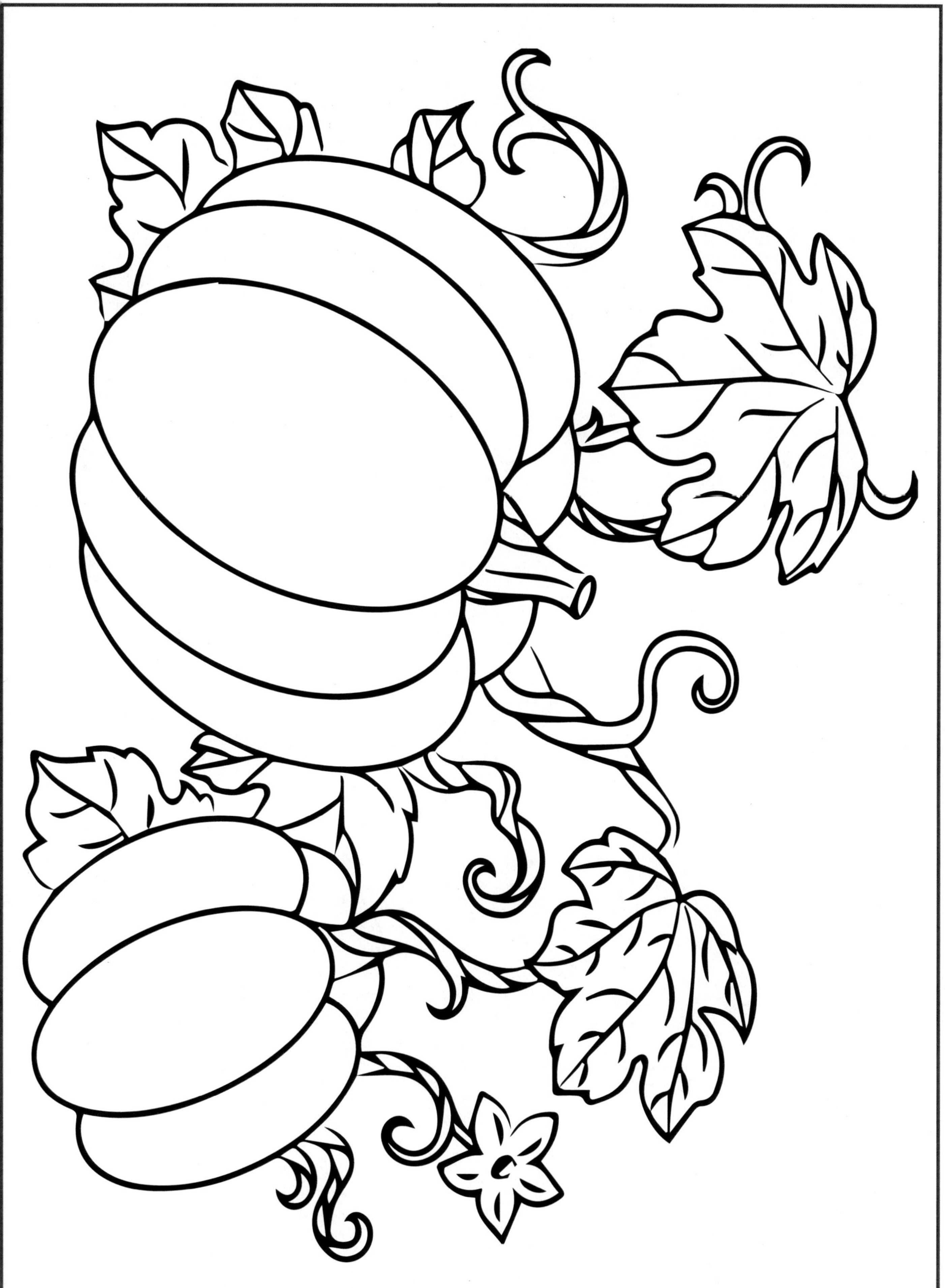